# SELECTED POEMS

for Pablo
whose traces can be found here

# Steve Griffiths

## SELECTED POEMS

SEREN BOOKS

**SEREN BOOKS** is the book imprint of
Poetry Wales Press Ltd.
Andmar House, Tondu Road
Bridgend, Mid Glamorgan



Cataloguing in publication data:
Griffiths, Steve
Selected Poems
I. Title
821.914

ISBN: 1-85411-088-8



*The publisher acknowledges the financial support of the Welsh Arts Council*

Typeset in 10.5 palatino
Printed by WBC Printers, Bridgend
WBC, Bridgend, Mid Glam.

**Cover Art: Carlos Torres 'Fragmentation'
Mixed Media on Paper 67x50 cm. 1993**

# Contents

*from* ANGLESEY MATERIAL (1980)

NEW POEMS

## *from* ANGLESEY MATERIAL (1980)

# Patchworks

of Amlwch,
a pattern of fields and buildings
interlocking with lives.

I have chosen
a folk pattern,
forsaking isolation

an interminable quilt,
joined to responses and influences
in conflict and agreement
changing subtly with changes in history
the growth of poems
the retreat of peoples
personal defeat and victory.

I have chosen
the use of available material,
a feature of the passing of time:

first when the system of cymorth, mutual help
precluded the need for a Poor Rate
in the unbroken tradition of the farming hamlet
its innocence broken by copper

then through the mining boom
when a sympathetic priest
petitioned for the injured
to the agent of Lord Anglesey

and through the simultaneous trough of the wave:
*a hut full of naked children*
*destitute of all conveniences*
*and almost all necessities.*

a patchwork of rags to be coveted
under the threat of the red cloth badge
of dependence on the parish —
beginnings of the red menace in Wales:

in the wake of those years,
the visiting of the people
with a winter of cholera.

in the good times, neighbourly
hogs rooted at liberty in the streets.

now we have tourism, all the neat squares
the Tourist Board has sewn up most craftily.

Patchworks of Amlwch,
a pattern of fields and buildings
interlocking with lives.

# Expectations

## 1

a home town of moving lace curtains

expectations of my career
and a trustworthy stone.

I had to disappoint them:
soon described as 'the boy who's on drugs'.

figures that shaped me were incidental,
an island I left to my childhood.

I left the discomfort of adolescence carefully
behind the horizon, which advanced,

creating a personal landscape
much like that of others, depersonalised,

where I might find myself in control
with words especially that formed the sea

that defined the cliffs and turf and ploughed
field of the personal landscape.

## 2

the farmers bent over the profit and loss
of their Welsh Blacks, night and day,

would neither understand nor find this important;
no more would the chemical workers, toolmakers,

or even the Councillors of Amlwch: an indulgence
rarely shared, I am welcome to it.

I shall continue to swim, naturally,
in the complex, esoteric tributaries

that are useful to me, leading
supposedly to simpler perspectives

but now I mind that they are rarely shared,
a personal judgement that transcends censorship.

If I stand in a field
with nothing in my hand for the farmer,

my mouth full of his meat
the knife of the steelworker on my table

lip-service or condescension, irrelevancy
or disregard on my tongue

and the drugs of the chemical worker in my veins
then it is time I saw myself to be underemployed.

## 3

I come to a poetry of place

having seen the sensitivity of an elite:
it is in the small comfort of our minds
that we are important

in a culture of mutual congratulation
not in the eyes of the excluded
no matter how humane we think we are.

A small boy in rags who misunderstands
follows me, pointing derisively, out of my past,
throwing dried balls of particular poetry.

## The Mines in sepia tint

A man beats his wife on the mountainside.

Their shouts pierce the copper drumskin
of the coming storm: the earth of copper
the heather, the copper sky:

everything rumbles round inside the drum.

the man in a grey suit, white-faced,
his eyes shifting fast and nervous
copper copper copper copper the woman
outraged by my witness of her beating

my warning shout as I passed
and my feet pounded the veins of copper
across country: then, poised on thin white legs,
doubtfully angry, wet hair plastered on my forehead,
sixteen, not knowing what to do.

They gave me silent, heated looks,
and I ran on.

Later, I wrote a poem about the pylons on the horizon.

Often I have written the wrong poem.

# The Horse's Mouth

On such a day among the stones and the shafts
among such shouts I could hear the eightpenny women
sorting the ore from the rubble for a pittance
at their long trestles with their hymns of the Revival

which for the most part effectively regulated behaviour
but for the corn Riot of 1817
when grain was still exported from Anglesey
though there was famine:

*nightly assemblages of persons*
*amounting to nearly 200*
*have kept the inhabitants*
*in a continual state of alarm*

the anonymous title of *persons*
thus distanced from the interests
of *alarmed inhabitants;* the *persons*
of course were egged on by *ringleaders*

who were brought to justice,
having *detained a vessel in the port*
*laden with corn, alleging its scarcity*
*in excuse for their conduct:*

on receiving a six month sentence
they were *very properly and very ably*
*admonished from the Bench;*
the troops embarked for Ireland again.

Imagine the loyalties of eightpence a day
to the Cornish managers off the tall ships,
the torn hands and the powerful forearms,
a yellow handkerchief knotted at the head.

Imagine the loyalties of eightpence a day,
the wages deducted by the Agent of the Mine
paid directly to the shopkeeper Greathead
his son-in-law, to encourage continence

and frugality among the labouring classes
*who are not aware of what you and I*
*understand as moral guilt,*
and filial profit:

*I fancy I have as great a feeling*
*for a poor man as anyone, but justice*
*to the concern demands severity at times.*

# Fruits of Virtue

## 1

Out of a descended generation,
a whore of the construction boom
pushing a pram, her eighteen year old
limbs white and thin.

when the engineers followed the money
and the power stations across the straits
the one spontaneous brothel was closed.

those who plan economies with the carrot of boom
and the stick of depression do not consider
the meaning of stable development

perhaps they should ask her, and in Welsh, too.

## 2

There was another we teenagers called *hŵr*
with the vaguest idea of what it meant
but well and secretly aware
of the weaponry of a jealous word —
respectably married now
for having been single-minded
about her man.
Her little perfect features
screwed up into her shout for him
at the door and the window
as he hid, which was his destiny
and his right, his weakness and his cunning.
We watched, and could not even speculate:
only repair the door later.

# Out of a descended generation

labouring at sixteen,
Austin Healey Sprite at eighteen
by the ruined harbour warehouses.

Then Fridays, Whitbread by the crate
overrunning the counter:
pints downed in under ten seconds,
a record of seventeen pints a night.

The construction boom paid for it
and left Amlwch high and dry after five years:
the power station fully automatic
the unemployed in the white light
of a sunlit empty square

boys that went to school together:

one, pointed out to all comers across the years
in the reflected glory of a month
on bass for Rory Storm and the Hurricanes
with Ringo Starr in the early days:
he leaned against a wall,
rarely spoke but watched the buses leave,
had a small family at home, and a guitar;
others, footballers, of the only privileged class
(apart from the managers and shopkeepers
with their tenners and wives in the cocktail bars)
the real heroes of the school to the kids of the tribe
their Saturday blazers and clean,
greased hair to be emulated
who treated the teachers with a gangling negligence
protected little selected kids,

abandoned others to the pack
and joined to ostracise with irrelevancy
the smooth-collared English
who talked of being graded with their parents' approval
and left at the first opportunity.

But big Wyn, with his glazed baby eyes,
being chased round the cloakroom by the other kids,
punched in the balls, doubled up
never losing his fixed smile
a target for the smallest fish of all
his arms flapping with distress

big Wyn sweeps the roads—
all have a kind word for him.

## Craig-y-Don

Nineteenth century foundations
lie under the skirt of a post-war estate,
distanced and softened with ivy
near a deposit of old prams.

# Courting prosperity

All legs and arms and grin
the sheer length of him
made his friends conspicuously small
teeth spoiled his profile
and his hair was wrong.

But coming from Liverpool
he knew how to be tough and quick at the same time
and the rumours that he carried a knife in school
made him a phenomenon,

quickened our readiness
to respond with a tense affability.
Round him grew a swaggering band
of country cousins, a not-so-comic hierarchy
of dogs, each knowing an exact fear that placed him.

All frequently used their combs.
Cross one, and from the next rung up
this threatening face would thrust in yours, cock-quick,
the skin stretched from cheek to neck.

The only thing they respected
was what they understood.
Juvenile bravado, black eyes, spat hate,
heads hammered into outhouse walls, all
hardened the edges of the galactic empire

to sustain the decadence
of legs and arms and grin,
who became untouchable in the space
he'd made to perform his mellowing.

He talked to sophisticated girls
from other rungs a social class above,
who were not so chic that they weren't impressed.
He disposed of his military history
in the lap of a soft-skinned college girl

who lowered her academic sights
and for a while continually undressed.
He learned the ingenuous satisfaction
of cattle among the gifts of the fields.

He became a farmer by marriage, with a past
to be laughed about with neighbours, affectionately,
with an old man who was thankful,
and a wife who understood crops and poultry,
drawing a curtain of hedges around them.

## Suffering does for the character

On the storm's wet tongue, greens,
mounds and tees are ground to perfection.

The professional watches, bald,
snug and pocked, in fluorescent plastic.

Little Titanic of a golf club dance:
the lights seen, now lost, fragile as a trawler

viewed from a dark promontory among the rollers:
gossip in evening dresses at a slight elevation

projected into the howling black.
Small businesses are made here,

in the pauses between the taking of cues.
The Dublin Packet has cleared the Stack.

Have you ever tried running against the Atlantic?
The aspirin sun swallowed hard at the horizon,

I have seen the Packet surrounded with green
menacing light, the clouds heaving like passengers,

running against the Atlantic, its ears flattened.
The turbines drumming the comfort of power:

the plastic cups in the buffet and the ring of the till
a statement in the hollow of enormity.

Like lived-in leather, like the skins of seamen,
struggle ebbs the mailboat to its worn beauty.

Beaten on rainy mountainsides by west winds
that follow the contours of erosion and recreate them,

so many people bear this quality: beaten women,
dark rings under their eyelids,

told this, too many children,
told that, too many winds

tugging at their coat across the bone: it is easy
for those whom force has never struck to scintillate.

A woman in a queue at the social security knows this,
seeing herself in the window of a coffee shop,

her image laid over a man with a tie
who leans forward animatedly to make his point.

He leans back, leaving precise ash on a glazed finish.

# Oil Terminal

## 1

### Comings and Goings

I think he was a shipbuilder
he wore an immense cap over one eye
he walked the morning pavements
lending them stability,
a pipe gripped in the right side of his jaw
his eyes very blue, watery with age and the sea;
a cared for look about his tweed
and an air of great content.

Pierre Cardin picked up his cap:
now it is worn by fashionable women
on holiday here; John Lennon
took the National Health glasses
with subtle and expensive alterations.
I used to think of him as the builder
of an Ark, patient, knowledgeable.
His craft with wooden ships has died with him here.

The lock gates are rusted and photogenic,
the slipways are grass.
Nostalgic engravings of full sail
entering the busy harbour
are sold by a local artist.
As the debate blew around the streets
there was talk of a marina,
compensation for an offshore oil terminal

which has arrived.

## 2

A collision of two objects, one moving,
the terminal is happening to the town.
For a couple of years, the labour force
is a resource, which means an object
in the planning of profits,
capital and oil are monopoly spaces to land on,
the game is set up with the mothering landladies
of the port, bemused by the incidental benefits
of bronze lodgers, divers and tugmen, windfalls
who will vanish when what is happening
to the town passes on like a shower.
Structures are imposed in the guise of gifts.

And the miners last century were given
the system of bargains, where they competed
by public auction for sectors of the working
and the lowest tender won, the lowest
outlay for the company, a gift of subsistence
and unemployment for the defeated rival.
Structures are imposed in the guise of gifts.

People outwitted and by-passed
by riders of the system's profitable crests
might have created a different wave
but then it is too late,
it is just oil on the water.

## 3

A million small points of chopped and moving sea
catch momentary metal-reflected
sunlight at their peaks, at the foot
of the rusty, tilted platform of the floating crane.

Workers guide the iron shoe of dredged ballast
for the breakwater as it sways on the jib.

By the old jetty's streaked welcoming
of local stone smeared with seaweed,
a child's game of construction,
cost-effective numbered concrete blocks
are hoisted and rearranged.

Old women with foam-coloured hair work
through the motions of bright washing on the line
at their square house, surrounded by the waiting
blocks, an alien intelligence, administered
by a Portakabin from Rotterdam.

The track to their house is dangerous to the
unauthorised.

To the east, ponies run on the clifftop,
the throb of machinery follows us to nothing,
pre-Cambrian outcrops into the rugged sea.

By-products of chlorine are lost in the blue air,
mossy rivulets swallowed in great churns of salt;

a curlew echoes back to us, wailing past a rock face,
oyster catchers dart in unison on the dark water.

There is a tanker approaching the point in the haze
like a white vision; I catch the drift of its engines.

# Llangefni Market

## 1

### The Bull

A black bull of enormous power
stands in its solitary pen
An inconceivable quantity of muscle
governs its mass.
It makes a bass, husky groan of sympathy
to a beef-cow in a nearby crowded enclosure,
throaty and demoralised, at the second attempt.
Its strong, gentle face: the black curls
of a solid Grecian deity.
The eyes of danger and deep water.
The mesmeric stillness, slow blinking.
We wonder at its marvellous career,
the balls slung low like footballs;
small townspeople shaken
by the industry of the carnivores, ourselves.
The rolling eyes of the smell of death.

A farmer passes, on first name terms with the bull.
It ignores him. He criticises the shortness of its legs.
I say, 'They've got a lot to carry', feeling ignorant.
'They won't have after today', he says with satisfaction,
and we walk away, to the next pen.

2

## The Café

There are many great wellingtons in the café today,
a masculine air among the housewives.
A stockman sits beside us with a shy grin,
almost a sheep's mouth twist, full of teeth.
blue eyes not right indoors, meant for wind.
He stares ahead, gripping his teacup
in his thumb, saying 'oh aye':
he twinkles into the middle distance.

A year ago today, it was all finished:
they fought the import of Irish cattle
when they could only give their own away
for the meaning of glut is disaster for them.
The farmer gets three times that price for beef now.
They changed the rules because of the song and dance.
'Oh aye, it's very good now' he nods
and swallows his tea to return to the market's rich smell.

# The Anglo-Welshman and his friends

To celebrate the culture would have been foreign to me

not least as there would have been
little truth in the exercise:

fighting parochialism at seventeen
the answer lay, it appeared, in the cosmopolitan
which became the rootless.

But there were certain formations of cloud
that change the colour of the landscape
and the temperature of the spine;

and the sea licked at my doorstep
or beat its virile chest, threshing,
taking a vigorous bath in its own bay.

The second families of the trawlermen,
the sea's moods were my friends.
I lost them in the cracks of city pavements,

cultivated others that have taken their place now.

# Under Mynydd-y-Tŵr

## 1

The mediaeval young made Sunday pilgrimages,
blessed at four stations of the island, every July.
We see them in a Victorian looking-glass:

a straw-hatted crocodile of picnickers
picking blackberries after the cricket,
mildly spiced with the ruffian charm

of Morris Men, shuffling out their dreams
self-consciously, in car-parks.
Peel this vision away with the other films

and we are left with a ritual power that will turn
and snap chaste fingers at the knuckle:

twenty 'virgins' in a dance to exhaustion
in honour of Brig, for valour and fertility.

Their songs are clinging brambles, gritty,
foul-mouthed with un-Christian energy.

It never paid to mix it with the spirit of summer.

2

## Milk Nosed Out

on the mountainside, a late lamb
surges up into its indulgent mother.

3

Seventeenth-century Venuses:
jumbled bulges of cumulus recline

along other, bluesmoke mountains
with icing, by seaboard blue.

Battered sea-pink survive between
the poxed and flinty buttock of Tŵr

on Môn's edge,
and the lavatory of the sea,

where herring taste
the regional delicacy

of Rio Tinto's cathode carbon waste.

4

## Mona's Owners

Iron Age hollows of soft grass.
Bracken, blazons of gorse.

Innocent hollows, tolerated
by the legionary: superannuated communes.

how could they live
without walls and mosaic aspirations?

A ragged ineffectual priesthood, too close
to the turf: its circular homes and songs

have always existed, touched to conscious use
by a minuscule timespring of history:

distanced by wind, strangely ennobled
by filth, and outflanked by a literate efficiency.

# Crossing Lady Stanley, here, 1868

You are ensconced in your vain folly
on the cliffs. The wind would flatten
even your hair, Lady Stanley,
posed with your frilled infants.
Before dinner you imagined yourself
to be Byron, stripped of his laughter,
self-glorified in a sunset of madness:

the cries of seabirds fell on each other
as so many colours fall at the horizon,
not considering the one below
shivering and settling in the shadow
of its transformation.
Now giant winds and giant darkness
outpower the tinkling cutlery of a family feast.

Your eyes illuminate the fat candles,
a manservant attends, and a mason or two,
for you want us to know what you did with all
that money:
your name is everywhere, benefactress of hospitals
and churches; purveyor of lasting graffiti,
Kilroy of the marble halls. Superseded
by Amlwch bootboys in rainy bus-shelters.

Last week, my friends probed your folly
and craned through your poor mock slits.
Lax feet turned the bean-tins in your monument,
half-curious, cameras in cases.
My face a necessary mask in a cutting wind,
I was laid flat in the heather; framed
in banks of cloud lay a lake of purest turquoise.

You stood at the edge of the colour, slight,
but there, as by the ballroom floor you might
have wanted to impress some well-lined beau.
Our minds moved together, a moment shared.
You would have shuddered at the intimacy.
You had bought this view. A carriage waited
on the mountainside, to remove it from you.

I carried our intimacy back to the van,
a fragment of eggshell,
a peasant savouring the illicit
with a little smile of gratification.
Your driver too was waiting,
with his patient, leathery face,
an impenetrable landscape.

# Getting it wrong, again

Photographs, fading already, recall my discomfort.

Choristers were allowed to faint, and we did,
guards falling out honourably on parade
with a sense of our place in a world picture.

I did it too often, the honour was lost,
replaced with an inured suspicious sympathy;
the customers' eyebrows raised to heaven.

I played to the gallery with my voice,
I thought I had class. My solace
was the tender attention of illness.

Times change, and pretended positions
are recognised or lost; I am gummed in the present,
undefended from the past.

So many others are more resourceful,
they have invested in safe houses
and a repetitive future free from pain.

When the sun is shining,
they will not put their umbrellas away,
then they deny the existence of rain.

I might have followed, but again I got it wrong
and when out scavenging half-heartedly for bricks,
the heavy showers made my hair grow long.

There I am, leading the massed choirs into the wrong stalls

at a celebratory service; at my back, the tall son
of the gardener, angrily poking me with his hymn-book,

in the scrubbed, anonymous line of distant faces where I belong.

# Taking Shelter

a sensual heat on the heavy leaves
luxuriating Llaneilian under Mynydd Eilian

the church pricking the hard brightness of the summer
since Patrick walked this land, influencing leaders.

later the English appropriated the church
and the Welsh moved elsewhere, with such

items of culture they could carry.
still a heat of visions in the yellowing graveyard,

an overgrown place, for fornication.
the nave, a cool dark island:

a skeleton painted black on the twisted gallery
a small coffin at the foot of the tower

flutes and pipes in a glass museum case
shattered, something struck it,

the splinters in the aisle; the birds and myself
nervously stricken in the porch.

the stone flaking slowly at the gate
on other time-scales.

onrush of cars headed for the beach
the wind sways the bushes to silence

it is time to go down there slowly myself
the glass, dust, and rounded wood in my mind

and the painting of Eilian and his fixed eyes and his six
fingers, giver of power and a name to this place.

at the beach, my teeth sink delicately
in a Midnight Mint, turning it slowly on my tongue.

kids throw a ball over a sleeping labrador.
the full car park brighter than any sea.

looking at girls with their reddening legs
to dismiss them before they dismiss me.

walking home alone through the hawthorns.

# Cemaes Songs

1

One image of success
was always to outdo
the dragons of repression

a girl of fourteen
forbidden the barbecue
by her father the minister —

I remember her laugh and her touch;
a sharp unfulfilled memory.
I was seventeen.

I think she played the violin.

2

The ruddy cheeks, the bright eyes,
not wine, but whisky,

an unconscious classical pose:
a boy, a drunk scrum-half
on a rock, looks at the horizon.

A transistor competes with the hush of the sea.

The hands plashing, the squeals
of the naked swimmers:
bathsounds, half-echoed, innocents.

3

The morning's incredible clarity:
the sea could be ruefully subdued,
but its one eye glitters still.

The refuse man with his bag picks his way
along the tide-edge, bending at intervals.
The aftermath of a party, nothing stale.

# Hymns and Backward Glances

## 1

### Christmas Night

Like the clear sound of crushed snow underfoot,
my pen hangs on the immediate past.

A muffler of wind wraps round the sturdy caravan.
Shadows of raspberry canes in my mother's garden

fall across my thoughts. Stars are laid out
in their impeccably timed wait for my emergence.

I am part of their systematic map.
Snows of clarification, newsreels of memory

cover my lines. By morning
there are new impassable hills, new transparencies.

2

**At the Consecration**

The wind warningly tugged
our starched surplices
in the stream of evening sun;
the Bishop of Bangor strode at our head
with his golden mitre to the House of God,
solidly, and belted the door.
Given admittance, we took to the aisle,
trying not to wobble as we walked
but to move as on Lewis's escalator
in Liverpool, with single-minded symmetry.
The wind rose. We sang, impressed
with the ritual electricity. The wind rose.
Big Chris got episcopal dispensation
to relieve his bleeding nose.
The darkness thickened, the wind
strained at the windows, a door at the back
broke open. Four men heaved to shut it.
Our wide eyes swallowed our concentration,
our faces burning, our music sheets stirring.

Creak of cargo shift.
Smallness of the collective voice
struggling through the service,
for those in peril on the sea.

Suddenly in the roof a skylight crashed,
the church was filled with a mighty rushing wind
from a square of blackness
that sucked us towards it.
This was the Consecration.

After God had visited,
I did not understand how so holy a man
as the Bishop could discuss the weather
with the organist.

Morning.
Every boat sunk.
An amazed, exhausted silence.
The wind still rushing determined
to compensate for its vacuums.

## 3

Returning, I live with a huge space
at my shoulder
and a light step.
A bird is a white arc
whose call forges a slit in the dome.
Memories and future pour in.

A rabbit, its eyes and ears swollen and senseless,
lollops across our path, now it can die.

These elements have coincided:
now the sea has lapped these fired grains
we can act or die.

The sea fits the coast precisely from moment to century.

My mind fits the strong exhalations of the surf.

Patterns of history, smallest events
in the folding of mountains.
Someone loses a satchel.
He reappears in a teashop, fulfilled,
his wife smilingly pregnant.
Names from my class
appear on competition charts
on the wall of a bar-room.
I pass through, my significance is
a commercial transaction for bitter.
My eyes alive in the fingers of time,
powerless as the sheep beaten into pens at the market.

In the port, a man eats chips casually
in the wheelhouse of the oil terminal tug,
among the deaths of landscapes and crafts.

Tired empty accidents give form to the future.

People with shit on their hands labour
with their capacity to change

their sharpest perceptions half-lit
and half-blinded with shit.

To make progress is not to play in the light
but it is to choose the light

to leave no energy unturned
in the darkness of history.

Our minds are cleared with the water of sources.

May the trees bend and spring back.

## *from* CIVILISED AIRS (1984)

# News of a Marriage

The world's reflected smoothly in our eyes,
as I would smooth your hair,
anaesthetised.

Everyone's in love, muffled
in the magic wool of couples
or out of love already

in a shoddy cloth of quarrels
over the shining pots
of the domestic mysteries.

Away from the carpeted landscape, they say,
some people move as quick as fish
with the urgency of survival:

a lot of people have left on planes
some with good reason;
some are back

their suitcases crammed
with views of cities
and disappointments.

In the hollow silence of the carpeted landscape
we stand, each muttering a childish apprehension.
The stairs are mildewed with darkness.
You can imagine but you can go no further,

frightened of the news that never changes,
yet still might:
spontaneity belongs to others now,
the point in the campaign where the desertions begin.

# Wedding photograph

The sun attacks in white on the reef outside the window.
White shimmers line the sharp rocks.
The soft blue sea behind the potted plant conspires.
A buoy or an ashtray hovers in the lagoon.

In the foreground, which is black
till the eyes are familiar, a couple
are getting married. Her flowers
and laughter rest lightly on the photograph.

The surf beats at the registry office window.
A starfish is dying in the rank sun.
The pool on the reef is translucent,
greener than wet baize.

They begin by naming themselves.
It is not just a postcard.
The rocks are sharp,
the indented sky insists on their line.

# Everyone watches the sunset

Everyone watches the sunset
in airport lounges waiting, groups that compose
themselves and rotate, clutching souvenirs and small change.

I carry your rough sparrowquick laugh
from the small hours,
bars of copper light from your fine hair.

In the train that carries you away
among clusters of words thrown casually
together like exiles

I could be the sound of chaffinches beyond the window,
the shadow on the carriage wall,
wearing your hat.

# A few bars over again

The surfaces of childhood give off a faint
light that lures us to our obsessions:

this adult too self-important
to stop slapping his big wet threshing fish
of words across the retreated room,
watched by a child who will always now
be poised in a half-open frustrated silence

this village festival too perfect
for the surrounding years,
a mirage in time towed on a string
through the shoals of disillusion
and the demands of family closing in

this blinding light full of motion
brimming with plankton and fire
this concentration the purer
for being merely physical, over the shallow pool
with a fine net, shadowing transparent prawns.

We catch ourselves playing over
these moments, a few bars at a time
without touching the keys.
We learn how to paint the sky
in a thousand ways

without ripping through to the original.
Your villages of painted clay lead sinuously home,
this series of windows penetrated
by an experimental light, this green against
blue that records a path overgrown or a strong dream,

this innocent wall against which
people are never lined up and shot
or if they are, the sky-blue wall
is defiled like chance leaves with the quiet
spatter of primaeval atrocities.

Then the need for a real house and a real
child crosses the old light.
Smears of an earthly innocence deepen
in your shadow, proscribing the past
like the light brush of a vapour trail

on a pre-industrial morning.
You move upstream, motors open,
languages falling off you like sweat.
Houses call out from within you
to be given form and firmly ripen.

# A Spanish providence

Under the muscled limbs
of the flowering chestnut
you coil, snoozing
near to the roots
and the follicles where I begin.

I look up through the serpentine
branches, and fingertunnels
and green bottlenecks furnish
scented rooms whose
flowered paper shifts soothingly.

You seem to have spun down
through these folded vistas
from the little spoiling
solicitudes for butter and cream,
security, best lace and frivolity

that cushion you, peeping
and smiling as a child
in a post-war Austerity photograph
out of a garden
resplendent and delicate.

Gah-gah, you say,
secure in the knowledge
that the opposition
has been eliminated.
A vigorous blade

on a bare hill
Daddy smiles the victor's
casual, masculine smile,
thrusting out of the stubborn
privation of war.

Daddy is vindicated:
now he takes lengthy siestas
and talks of reconstruction.
Mummy is beautiful.
She passes round the olives.

In your next picture,
your first communion,
you make a run for it
bored and sweaty
in your biting petticoat

setting the stamp on your future.
Under the veil, your mother's glance
of fire: the firm hand laced
with exquisite piety:
the nip of her fingernail.

With its loving dedication scored through,
on the following page I found
a portrait of insupportable beauty
with a little narrow triumphant smile
that knows there's never long to wait:

a couple cut into relief, one holding
the scissors blindly, one adoring without a sound.

The moments are thrown on the table,
the possessed faces
called into formation.

You join me in some terminal, as always
like a closing of unnatural spaces.
Teenagers queue at the picture kiosk
with lovely assumptions of poise.
You're clutching the empty faces

of a prisoner with the bitter innocence
of a foreign girl in a foreign town
where hands reach out from the shadows
and nothing moves but a tape
left running over tense-lipped silence.

There are so many words for you
and I am constantly grasping them,
as many nervous eyes on history,
so many botanical terms never
known in a massive English landscape.

You pass by, breathing life into mirrors.
This time I touch you, a small
unknown moment, a small unidentified
flower verging on the miraculous
but particular, and asleep under great trees.

The galleons drive through the channel
with so many powers and fragilities.

# Still too quick to hold

The bus driver
went gently on the bends.
My son moved with the delicate swell.

A technician in dull green
scans your mound
like a vase to be dated.

All corners,
an apprehensive Gawain
at the foreseen tumulus,

I wait for the marvellous green child
to leap into view,
my instruction, my inheritance.

You lie there like someone
on the news who would like to be watching
as well as making it

and the baby's born momentarily,
a restless green sonar blur
swimming onto a screen,
refusing to pose, in absolute confidence
prodding the interior toys of mother
who will not forget, giving
bloodily under curious fingers,
one with fish and the birds of the air:

*here in the belfry hangs the heart*
*here the lungs, here the musical stomach*
*and the watery sack they bring me in,*
*and the lifeline to thrust aside,*
*swimming dangerously.*

The baby leaps against the air
like a persistent salmon
rippling under the element
of my laid palms.

Beyond, over there, the haze
of time, the mountains of love,
unconcerned, apprehensive, unconcerned
warming like damp turf an hour after dawn.

# Courage

My baby's harelip's darned brilliantly
like the hospital sheets he lies on.
Others wait for the train
back from the seventies,
where infant mortality grows
like a lump on the breast.

Wards close
and the nurses grow fierce, unnoticed.

Arms outspread in splints,
cherub or bird, his gums are bared
as his mother, his dependable
aviary of mobiles, and his father
move the other side of his tears.

His blood is bright as an old man's,
the incision part of my acute past.
Nerves run crying to my shoulder
when I think of it,
with an anxiety pale and grubby
as a sleepless father
wearing the badge of his lip
as he walks through my dream,
eyes and hands alight, chuckling
at his mother who leans over him
in a little storm of generosity.

The baby grins briefly
at his own strength
through his pain,
the first mirror.

## Small substantial shadow

Our living proof that provokes the cat
to violence with love.

In a plastic mac with the sleeves turned up
he points at the rain
making dashes on the lake's dark screen.

Little maker and unmaker
his bed's a bazaar, like Pharaoh's tomb,
he can sleep on a book or a helicopter.

Little creator or destroyer,
he's our tender confluence
shouting and running in the hall:

a stone thrown out of our lives,
twisting away through the air
like a discus out of a stadium.

Our neighbours know it's the throwing,
the exuberant fling of the arm
with him, more than direction,

leaving the chaotic distant kisses blown,
rosepetals, the cigarpuff of a reporting gun.

# From Waterloo Bridge, ensuing dark

among the multitudes
Of that great City, oftentimes was seen
Affectingly set forth, more than elsewhere
Is possible, the unity of man,
One spirit over ignorance and vice
Predominant, in good and evil hearts
One sense for moral judgements, as one eye
For the sun's light.

Wordsworth, *The Prelude*
Book Eighth, ll. 823-830

My nose angles the air,
a little missile edged into the sunset,
little receiver, the indigenous one
who doesn't belong,
sensing an odour of fascism
round a lack of generosity,
like the swelling round an inoculation
gone wrong.

Newspapermen prowl the dusk
attacking strangers,
ribbing out their flesh
which hangs in colours on the line
to warn of habitation and strict ways.
In the ensuing dark, queues form
for doctors.

Through the civilised airs of Islington,
Schubert floats by an open window
with greenery.
Within, the authenticity of taste,
its dull sheen.
There are some who would believe
anything for this.

In a community centre
bandaged with posters,
civilisation deepens in a way
undreamed of where the river, trembling,
licks at the stanchions
where a ticket costs more than a child
on social security,
a little indulgence,
the hoarding of heritage
at the South Bank.

This old communal laundry fought for,
the washing-slabs gone
with grandmother's solid arms;
then control of it,
playgroups fought for,
the children melting down
hundreds of partitions.

Here are the ovens of capital,
swarming with warmth.

# Consequences

With hungry old eyes,

like a plant in a cupboard, a woman
looks at the movement of light through the street.

She picks up the roar of Ocean, towering
over the suffocated Fleet,

broadcast urgently from the Stadium
(every blow a blow for Stardom)

the hiss of collective breath
drawn at a disappointing miss.

Her sight falters
like an uncleaned window:

she watches the air thicken
on her three yellow roses.

Some of her arteries
throng with laughing voices:

there's Mum and Dad with a boy on leave
seated at the piano, singing lustily.

She knows the gestures of the cats.
She watches a black family.

Sometimes, the cries from the Stadium
reach her a fraction ahead

of the cries from the radio.
Anger is their predilection.

Sometimes, her dinner gone cold in her lap,
buried mirrors in wardrobes quietly pulse.

Bailiffs claw at her window
waving the final red demand.

As we see them, in a series
of frames identical yet unconnected,

all the old women she knows
merge into one, a dark mass

over the children on the terraces,
unloved and vicious.

She rehearses the songs unwritten.
Here are the well-scrubbed floors,

here are the taking hands unbitten
here the babies guided between the doors.

The mouth drops open and the eyes burn
with pleasure at the thousand scarves
and the rhythms of the floodlit twilight.

The losing side obey the laws.

# Shrinking horizon

In a public darkness
private stars glimmer behind a curtain.
Darkness pours at the windows
off buildings close by.

If I retired to watch
the brighter moments at a distance
I would seek myself out in exile,
accused of dereliction.

They are closing the children's wards,
they are breaking up the future.
A pile of agendas
in a buzzing, dirty twilight.

We slide back the decades
to the big stones on the roof of the moor.
I sit watching them
with my small clerical hands,

Stonehenges that never transcended
the weather's disorder.
The lean wolf's breath on the white neck
guarantees a tomorrow.

# Post imperial

Reggae thumps, a hangover,
fruit and meat drumming the ground
in a thunder from the imperial past.

An elm stands like a fishbone in midsummer.
The cats fornicate in its barbed shadow,
the lean strays motored for lust.

The sweat-shops are gutted,
their staircases hung like tongues.

A bank signals from the city,
the counting-house to the bare threshing-floor,
the Christmas light to the vacated room.

The moon hangs in the elm
like a hat hung on justice.

A man waits for a bus that never comes
there are drunks drunk with waiting
for history as it goes past their noses,
rolling unevenly like a ball on the cobbles,
there are drunks starved of the evidence
in streets full of ghosts.

The puzzle of development,
the groan of human industry
heave the landscape into a straight line,
assisted by wind and war,
dogshit and cartons on vacant lots,
used durex and rubble, the refuse of casual acts.

# Hairdresser, age 55, Dalston

Terraced streets, her intricate perms
rippled across the greying heads,
mortared with lacquer.

Her house was a ship into another world.
Skinheads rucked past her draped lace curtains
leaving a smudge on the air,
high on aeroplane glue,
running feet, swung pipework, thuds
that vibrated the window-frames like a truck.

The humming ranks of driers,
the tang of shampoo,
her royal texts,
the husbands at the threshold, there to collect.

Her incorruptible trinkets,
her white arms working.
Her dust-sheet silence,
her practised chatter along rails.
Her canyons.
Her kindness to children.
Her close things.

I heard a delicious solitude,
soaping itself, in her lonely bathsounds.
The white, wrinkled pore-stars of her imagination
a white bear undiscovered, echoing
contentedly in a white pool.

And I see her taking vengeance
on what others have made:
the bent necks of the skinheads
under the rod of her avenging alabaster angel,
the Victorian terraced hillway to the pit,
their faces turned upward,
their arms laid aside,
urged onward by uniformed guards.

# Guardianship

Around the walls pebbled with violent glass
set in cement
to save values from vandals
the insomniac blood roams
like a fox watching fire
that comforts
fox-people with brilliant implements
and edgy thoughts.

*It is easy to see the provision*
*of any order as a saving grace,*
*my desk as a liner in savage lightless seas,*
*shedding the reassurance of its cabins' trim*
*on the gaping, clashing rooves of the waves,*
*cherishing the machinery,*
*the possible,*
*for want of another principle.*

*I do what I am paid to do*
*at my desk with my computer terminal:*
*they can rustle my outward papers,*
*the Vandals and Huns, when they burst in —*
*brimming with red-eyed fecklessness,*
*their cleavers flecked —*
*for I have inviolate information.*
*I have done relatively well.*

*They break the bulbs of neighbours' passageways,*
*strike out each others' eyes.*
*To abandon your luggage is a fool's game.*
*Observing the convention,*
*I do not speak of those who never had it.*

*Each is a radio in a lonely cubicle.*
*I read the morning papers with ferocity*
*to stem the snapping ideological tide.*

The blood puts its voice in a mixer,
crowds, buzzes.
It flows down to the hallucinatory green
of the pitch, like a spillage
wanting to eat the stars,
pawing them,
those cuts of meat left
upright in socks,
their fast convertible health,
a meat-eaters' carnival.

# Education

Old, mad, dancing Mrs Dean
celebrated the expiring candle
of her eighty years
with three kids from the estate,
whose harassing fingers
scrabbled like rats and draughts
in the space between door-frame and wall.

Bitten with inspiration,
she put a match to the crack.
A scream.
Next day they were back.

'Who shall I vote for?',
she asked me
when I told her she could,
'they're all smilin' 'addocks'.

Her ceiling came down
and her rent went up,
all caused by a man with a degree.

# Climber

Turning at every few thigh-straining pushes
on the steep soft slope, I feel
the years raise their backs,
effort by effort

and as the unobtrusive hills rise about me,
I hear tiny breakages in the wind
that mark time, small birds
clinking like glasses over the distant stream.

# Llantysilio, overgrown

Under the rush of caravans on the Holyhead road
and the thwack in the wind
of the campers' polythene streaming
and the hum of the scale-model traffic
on the miraculous bridges with realistic water below,
Tysilio's island hugs its cemetery to itself.

The graves are decked individually
as if each decomposition had its flower:
on dark slate, violet; the spindrift of the disappointed
lips cast from the cheekbone; and these delicate
heavenly ones, nodding at the mild Sunday air
after a lifetime stamped in the gasping furrow.

A green-armed bramble
lances the wind on a thousand tiny fronts
for the unremembered improvisor of hovels,
for tillers and singers, the little stone-skimmers:
a voice secreted over the mouths stained
with their own juices in their made beds.

# Children in a walled garden

The dreams are rare visitors now,
haughtily enigmatic, they know
the horizon's cemented in, though flawed.
Last week, in an airless visitation, a pair
of vicious and jaded politicians caught me
measuring furtively how many sheep
rank with dried piss and fear
would fill the intolerant volume of their car.

I see how freely my two-year-old
abandons his buttressed cities of lego,
a cat forgetting a mauled fly.
The airy mistakes of unsupported walls
cave in like the shrugged-off catastrophe
of ants under the darkening sky
of a ribbed sole on the lawn.

What a cheated irregularity,
what a deception of that foam
in the high wind from the rocks
is my painstaking accumulation of poetry,
bandaging and crystallising, guiding
the bones of a last Emperor's
concubine's bound feet.

I notice how eagerly
I follow your tricycle
on the faulted pavement
like a seagull after a tractor
in my old wild mint days,
viewed through a rough hedge on the hill
when the future was an overlapping
of headlands fading to haze.

# Geriatrics

Sun kings
their faces sagging like the combs of cocks

seated in splendour,
solitary and royal, beyond anger.

Red-eyed
old falcons in a bleak sunset;

talk to them?
It is an honour — they turn their heads

and look at you,
their conversation refined to the important pieces of the past

an exclusive school
of poets in striped pyjamas stained with urine.

Some, refined
to their wildest dreams, fathers of the tribe

they live behind a quiet
line of starched sheets, white seagulls.

Through the water jug
of a national assistance counter clerk

aged eighty-three
fluorescent lights quiver with rainbows

and lazy bubbles.
Then a slow haemorrhage on a seismograph, not recorded

in Los Angeles.
In another, enlightenment, plunged in a submarine valley,

echoes with colour,
azure peak, rings clear. Lightning:

the sun on a knifeblade
flashes across a cornflake packet.

Quiet museum burials
for the jewels and stone crosses of the unthought-of ritual

binding of the race by fire,
for mister death's fierce packed lunch of religious gimmickry.

They consider mildly
their unkept gardens which are also a kind of museum.

Awry and incongruous,
their power sits on them

staring blandly
at the sun as at children through glass.

A clinical nurse
hums a moment from a ballad:

phenomena become
disconnected in their own magnificence:

you forget the meaning of sounds.
You wonder if that was ever important.

# In the railway hotel at Cordoba

The sound of many running feet
down the corridors in waves.

I twitch like a dog hunting
asleep in the yellowing hotel.

Street rituals,
the people of Cordoba take on their true age
moving as an inquisitional congregation,
their eyes dark,
not to be distracted.

Suddenly hons wail from end to end
of the town they echo across the plain
and from wall to wall they clang shut on the present.

They travel up and down the length
of our restless bodies in the small hours.

They travel across other prairies
in the softened tones of harmonicas.

The movements of the congregation seep through
the walls,
they kneel and stand alternately.

Now I am in the corridor
in a tangle of foreign stations,
half-dressed,
walking to the stairs to take part.

Trains are arriving all night,
they discharge hurrying crowds
with lonely wails in which the private
thoughts of fascists are lost.

The incidental sounds of existence,
the marching songs of Moors and Romans on the high road,
the working songs of the women, creak of pump,
patter of feet, are the surest things,

and the train horn,

that empties you till there is only your pulse
and the sound of your breathing in the corridor,
and the yellowing floorboards

and the train horn,

that binds history into an unearthliness,
a key to the feeling of time displaced
in Cordoba,

where my few thoughts flutter like small anxious bats
in a well which is really the sky.

## Island with army, pines and wind

pine needles receive our bones
softest night in days

trees bend over each other
in attitudes of concern, grating their hands
with an underpatter, the soft dropping of cones

a car circles from military installation
to military installation,
passes an empty sentry in the rain.
the east is dedicated to military purposes.

interlocking lighthouse beams
search trunks for insects
at nervous intervals.

distant thunder, rattling of dry peas in tins,
rolling of boulders in globes.

bock, bock of radar.
bock, bock of unspeakable dreams.

Japanese wind chimes:
tinkle of steel rigging,
many pitches,
many little cymbals
and a low, subtle rhythm, three and four beats,
irregular intervals;
wind in steel mast
bamboo flute vibrated gently
in the hand of a master.
the wind counters with its moan
on the subject of nothing, unbeatable drums.

Unable to see our feet in the black milk,
we climb the hill that conceals the village.
the darkness is absorbed in its music.

# Contractions

1

The richest moment
is at the very beginning

    when all you have said is proved to be mere trickery
    the possibilities are endless

in the spring that tinkles from the stone mouth
you'll find the wearing down of a trawlerman's hands

    wedding-cake liners
    marshes of salt that die off into time and distance

2 for Jess

I do not want to prove things all my life.

I'd rather watch the foxgloves sometimes
deer at the skirting of the wood

    hoofprints in furrowed earth,
    proof enough.

the contour of hills, the contour of small stones.

## *from* **UNCONTROLLABLE FIELDS (1990)**

### Rivers are running beneath us

Cars line up over the buried Fleet,
agents of dubious liberty

riding on air,
tethered with gravity.

Below, a mole
noses the femur

of a long-murdered
Constable of Moorgate,

cudgelled in former
meadowgrass then

in one fluid move,
purse and throat slit.

Silvered, the grasses
bent their heads under the moon.

The wife never knew.
She haunts briefly:

the matter was not so deep.
Nothing hears

the mole's small cry
among the foundations.

# Glyndŵr Subdued

Burned out, there was no road back,
and the flames of Sycharth brought Glyndŵr
dreams enough:
his home was a country now,
the revenges multiplied.
The helicopter's shadow,
a great hare
runs fleetingly across a field —
the grass panicking, flattened,
trying to disperse but unable.

Almost an experiment,
the disciplined ructions of the first raid,
the strained respect for brawny lives
a delicate line: Rhuthun settlers,

robbed and dishevelled, emerged
to a heady, bright, small Welsh triumph
reeking of sheepshit
and soot in the bright sun:

insults counted, it was a homely,
small, scared, village altercation
as shoving and grunting skirmishes
around slag once made history.

The victors clattered away
shod heavily with expensive curses
to where even the sparks on the hill
were drunk down by the mud and the dark.

Later the conscripts, cast-off and dangerous,
sported their rusted dream of omnipotence,
hacking for their neglected fields
and their friends cut down,

and then for the riven cold in their bones
women ran in the wet grass
brought down like deer with cries of triumph.
People ran blindly,

made his, the pervasive guerilla
reeking of smoke and prophecy,
the peaceloving fire
displaced in his rafters.

The banging of shields,
plastic and leather,
rang in his ears:

war war war sle sle sle
went the childish wailing of sirens
in the gusting wood,

and the night's drunken instruments
scoured the wet streets
for the Welsh doggis and their whelps.

An English city listens behind curtains
to the running and breathing, the slugging
thud of quarry cornered and floored:

the resistance is
that we will not turn the television up
in tribute to the night.

Divided loyalties, undermined
meal-tickets, sprouted on hillsides,
the weeds Indignation
twined with deep-rooted Ambivalence

picked for the same dish.
Drenched resisters sidled in droves
along valleys to give themselves up
to the straggling columns of troops and grain.

When the fighting is over, the land of dreams
is a table lit with unshareable faces,
a once-in-a-lifetime
remembered meal to the hungry:

a looted peacock under the arm
of some big, sharp-featured
father of mine
who dried his eyes at the flame of Sycharth.

Then the withdrawal to memory
of the fair people, walled in the clouds
of exile within, the retreat to mystery
of the fair times on their vague upland tracks.

Glyndwr had to master this potent
trick of retirement, to the light
in a dolmen glimpsed rarely and late,
a light in the mind

where sometimes he lingers noisily in the grid of years
and the speed and charisma growl in him
to the applause of the shingle in the undertow,
old chimera whose wait has a tide's hypnotic

push still. It breaks
in like the sudden clatter of leaves
of a kneeling army

or a belief in the mountains upturned,
with mirrors,
lit from inside with our own light.

The poem uses the chant of the northern English students at Oxford, heard by Adam of Usk, at the beginning of the Glyndŵr uprising:

*War war war, sle sle sle*
*the Welsh doggis and their whelps.*

# Villa-Famès, August 1986

for Fernando Almela and
i.m. Alberto Solsona, 1943-88

Red, soft-rock strata cut a line
of niches, shelters, age-creases
and navels in dry, strewn terraces
of erosion and collapse.
In hardened powdery space
abandoned to hawks and foxes
we were easily scattered
among fossils.
Our voices indiscreetly
defied the undersea silence
among the winds, and were lost.

In a decorated overhang
a chipped half-circle of stick-men
move with serious staves and appetite
through layers of memory and smoke.
It's their blood inundates the streets
from flood-channels high in the town.
With an arrow through him
a bull rears and falls forward
in ochre and blood,
surrounded in the grey bushes.

The afternoon gone badly awry,
firecrackers, beercans and oildrums
crash through the last of the bull's mind.

Neatfooted, barrel-chested, tossing
star on a rope with a minder, he came in
to the faces leaning forward to applaud
and the leafing back of old men
in their irony and knowing pride
for boys their children raised
who stretch and thrust and crow
their hips seasoned with wine and panic.

Their fast trainers touch
the edge of the bull's reach
to provoke the girls with fingers sucked
between their teeth:

the bull keeps coming,
he's a boxer with the odds stacked
and the crowd applaud its dreams,
his breathing
sorely intimate and provoked.

He bursts up the stairs, over a barrier
scattering runners into back yards
breaking sanctuary.
Women wave red towels for him
and he looks for his escape in lizard cracks.

He's down again, quick and light
and goaded by the curious flapping of a hat:
he fills a gap between spars
with his jarring distended trophy of a face.
He leaves a last mark in the wall of a café.

Only his tail and flanks move
and a scribble of flies
that ride his heat.
There's a questioning
unsteady stillness.

Through a field that blossoms handkerchiefs
and hands to catch his eye, he turns
to begin his last passes
to the small men running away
down his long vista.

The halter's ready.
Behind him are stick-men who poke and shout.
A beercan clatters towards him.
A father holds up his little girls to the bull.

He's wound in closer on a line
towards the butcher's laundered shorts.

The murdered bull goes up to the square,
becomes hung meat on a cross,
is elected mayor and presides
over a music shrill, lop-sided, steely
with a movement of hips for his death.
There is subtle food in the clarinet and saxophone,
there are stately dark shades
on dining chairs, dressed for a nativity.
A slow colouring from the throat
of a trumpet hovers round
intimate parts that glisten in buckets
and probably reflect the stars above,
however faintly.

Six fiesta queens relax
beyond the arc lights, lounging
doe-eyed in their self-belief;
six official virgins off-duty,
marriageable somewhere between tonight
and the eighteenth century,
decorated with good hope,
strapping daughters in shawls
of intricate lace,
the village fixed on them
with carnival tenacity
to invest in and honour their vigour
of weathered figureheads
with green shoots and a lick of paint,
their grandmothers' gold combs in their hair.

Through flaking teeth of rock
that lay broken on hillsides
run imprints of movement,
rushes of stone, stills.

A lean fox turns to watch
women once honoured
bury the thin resilience
of their voices in ploughed land.

Dry clouds crackle their long storm
like a leaf in the fist
over a parched line of almonds.

*A video trained on coils of blue plumbing*
*in a bucket by the fountain*
*summoned the gut-stirring curiosities*
*of the Civil War:*

*those farmworkers who carried out*
*centuries of the bodies of saints and nuns*
*and arranged them*
*interestingly, in daylight*
*in the plenitude of their inheritance.*

Scavenging in the early chill of the square
the fox looks up to the silent windows
and the sleepers behind their eyelids of stone
where blood dries quicker than music.

# Elegy for John Tripp

A man on the radio talked of soft tissue
printed on million-year riverbed
like a morning-after mattress —
and I thought of you very clear, John,
lifting a pint of dark in some dolmen basement
regarding the sudden answers of the morning
after your stealing away, your sharp face
set in that spirit of mock astonishment
you learned to bewilder
producers of talks and tired assumptions.

I remember a belated urgency
in your face, as it turned back
watching the cultivation of soft edges,
as history, its fares paid, took off like that taxi
we tried to hail with a borrowed carafe.
There was a march full of friends' banners
and irony, probably sodden,
with a brass band and a cock-up somewhere.

On a stand in another world
the unprofitable take an unremitting review
of their leaders.
You take the salute, spilling drinks
and blood and atonement, and you break the silence
with what nearly everyone felt,
snarling at flummery, throned, waxing manic
then tender as warm buns in a paper bag
with some small forgiven fault
from your recognised gallery.

Confusion and moral astonishment,
something unfinished, an obvious instruction
unlearned: you listened and stirred tea
to the huge roaring ironies
of shopping bag conversation
as the rust-red deep shit rose at the window.

Then you slotted the poems accurately
in the darkness between laughing teeth
in darkened smokefilled rooms
like some young boy who, they said, had
'immaculate positional play';
like the occasional sun through the steamy
windows of your café,
illuminating the brown sauce and the salt.

And you planted your ground of demands
that you never sold
for one moment of narrow-angled comfort,
brambles round tanks.
Your green armies
knitted their sharp-eyed peace,
needling hard minds,
weaving, digging, planting,
still they work and plot:
they move down out of the hills' cover
laughing their experienced laugh.

# Continuity

I dreamed a tiger
in a suburban tennis court
pursued me with ominous grace
and quiet hunger.

The wraith of my son's hand
raised at my shoulder:
he had been eaten whole
but kept coming, a whiteruffed silence.

I ran, breathless
with that curious infant sense
of disembodiment:
I was the dead boy at my father's shoulder

gathering sinew in the corner of his eye
like firewood as it turned colder,
too keen
to be merely confined or devoured.

# Fathers

Animate and silent, columns of rain
wheel slowly off the mountain.

My friend sits twitching like poultry,
male tears hoarded, unlocked now
their late gold burns
then streams down to his five year
pull between warmth inherited
that had to be worked for, inhabiting history
like children asleep
after taking the day at a run,
and the roughshod and ridden, uncertain
power of gay self-discovery:
those boys' arses moving before him
buds and mirages grown substantial,
the familiar form in the dark bed
finally unreal.

Unable to touch his family,
the confused, unpardonable loving recoil
cauterised with guilt's daily charge.
He found no reliable words for the dark
encroaching, and the light bothered him:
the echo of trees on an empty lake
harried him back to the cliffs of mother.

On the day my father left us,
his barrel-chest brooked no question:
he directed the photographs and the trains
and the angle of the sun.

But although I was there,
I was too difficult to be snapped at four.
Later, held up on a bridge, the driven smoke
of another shining monster blasted my eyes.

When I was ten my mother told me
he must have died, and that was true
till the close old deity put forth shoots again:
those hidden years he'd compressed a massive
chord,
his round weight on the black-and-white keys
of the Bechstein he owed a student for,
a continuous layered humming inside me
till, all power and slowfired resurrection,
relic and animal,
he pawed at the lid and the brandy:
I was flung back twenty-five years
to the hesitation of four.

My friend drove with me to the shuttered village
of my grandfather and his unmentioned brothers.
Nothing happened
but a white horse by a stream,
a farm on a ridge
and a church without a roof.
The hawthorns pointed and waved
their freckled white
like airport spectators
at the harsh blue bearing down
till we covered our eyes.
An awkward visit, a warning.

We drove back through abandoned workings,
through an archeology
softened with explanation.
Throat full with his tearhoard,
in a dream my father tells me
it could have been so different,
his mute hands smearing the childhood ivory.

# Unmetalled Road

In memory of my father, 1893-1984, composer.

He went when I was four:
there were a few stamps from Africa
that bore the reassuring orange tree,
the one I believed money grew on.

Responses are grafted and trained
but they take their own curious flight:
ashes clouding the wind,
they become a shared thing,
a spilled thing.
Like cattle in churned mud,
the wreaths breathe on each other
in a corner of intimate sustenance,
lowing their silent farewell.

The past darkens and advances like a wall,
lightfooted creatures moving behind it.
Old and stooped, he knew the score
and it's buried and his,
music lingering like gas
or a secret body under an old floor.
His city reverberates in taut wood
and burns, it is long gone Belfast,
he takes it with him in a mason's box.

He creeps past my narrow bed
in the dark, looking at me with rare
tenderness among barks of prejudice,
a goblin with the rotating eye of a lighthouse,
a mastery of empty searoads.
The wall holds its breath.

He bobs by on the night
and I try to make of him
something less than a monster, small but imposing
appeared suddenly from far out at sea.
Damp-eyed reminiscence floats in, regrets
and boasts each hiding the truth like a room
viewed through glasses of brandy.

Old foghorn on full sail
he goes by grandly preoccupied
with his voices spread along Gothic ceilings
outward like palm leaves in cathedral spaces.

He leaves me with his unvisitable
crag of complaints and psalms
which stand in their own time:

making allowances for age and a thoughtless
and ruthless desire for only the best
I listen for the quiet haunting of his blood.

# The Guesthouse

In a living hold
of legs and table-spars
I hugged my knees and listened
beneath the long table-talk
to the creaking of seasoned joints,
the friction of thighs in nylons,
to my mother's nerve
carrying the spirit of the house
through the stir and grate of coffee spoons,
the guests diving for wit's minnows,
the spirit of the house carrying her nerve.

The past is swallowed, or crystallised
like laughter caught in the bottom of a cup,
to be washed out or examined
till the particles dance:
the trick pyjama-man hung from a light
who faced the sea in a darkened room,
the laughter that ran down
a sweating kitchen wall
like a thrown egg
or caught the skin like sea-holly
planted between sheets.

After the meal,
we ran with the dogs on the sand,
we knew nothing, suspended,
their pink tongues lolling at speed
past the washed-away gravehill.
Under the sea were the overrun stumps
of a forest, at low water
you could see the swimming heads

of bladderwrack
and this was how the forest of Welsh
drifted away perversely
on an incoming tide,
receding as the rafts crossed Menai,
a waterbird beyond the trees
striking distance and terror
in the invading troops
for this densely populated language
of fogs and yellow grass.
My dogs ran towards it,
barking to enter
through the long sealight,
from the bleached coastways
into the hard bark
and the leaves that drip
their stickiness into open mouths,
but there was nothing where they stood:
oystercatchers quivered their limit
in the tide-edge light.

We blushed with sweat,
spiky-haired and sand-encrusted
in the shop at the end of the beach;
we were tormented across the sweetjars
by some unattainable thing of
lace and fulsome violets,
her chaste Welsh poise
so very clean, our shyness intact
as tender breasts encased
in the firm imaginary government
that she exercised over us,

and we ran back to a vigorous system
of dams and canals
that we built and destroyed repeatedly
from a rivulet that leaked out under a rock
and spread across the sand to meet the tide.
We made a prosperous broad swathe
of yellow crops and minerals
with buried trees and relics,
full of small hidden scenes:

*here, a boy looked up at the locomotive*
*his father, refusing to be lifted up*
*to the footplate for the dirty*
*brilliance of the anthracite that burned*
*with integrity from every face,*
*and it rode away, taking its power*
*to be smashed in the waves;*
*here a boy waved a stick amazed*
*as the tall cattle sauntered like liners*
*under his power in deep mud*
*(here a group at the piano echoed*
*the suspended bite of good harmony*
*into gathered corners)*

and we yelled as level after level
of our world collapsed
beneath the waves that crashed and curled
over the clouded faces of the lakes —
you could see people running
on the listed decks of a steamer —

we yelled and rebuilt,
the sea at our elbow
sated mischievously
with ships pulled over in the night,
a great sow that smiled and fawned
in the adulterous shallows
that lapped the sand from under her nipples
at dawn, small waves purling over her.

Now, my creations lie about me
in a guest house room,
found and set out
as ornaments of porcelain and brass:
selected acts and losses,
the deceptions
that passed over my head
in a living ship of adults
with the dry pollen of cheek and groin
there among pods dropped
round a vase on a sideboard.
It could be a place of silent attrition
as downstairs the ghosts take tea.

On the cropped, wine-dark lines of the carpet
I push my Maserati to its limit:
how the tyres hold their bends,
the commentary's roared out
to a distant knot of voices
woven with radio choirs
on some bar of time, where rows
of mothers are calling us in late
from the dunes,

where the shell of a church
is sturdily beached,
little humblecake walled round
above the tidal rocks by a testing site,
pointing west out to the migrations.
In the shrunken timber of the door
high-coloured boys in uniform
have gouged and left their mark
beside the grated stones of the bay.
Small yearly services,
the rare flap of a cassock
hold on to a residual power in the air
by what remains of the causeway
there among the disordered shingle.
Turned on the sea,
the land's curved bowl reverberates
after the passage of a fighter.
I add my name and leave
pursuing dishevelled saints
in cauldrons of wind.

# Contact

She came up to him at closing time
among the hulks of breath outside the Cock,
hugging herself, too late
for the preliminary swift half
well understood among plenty.
'Where d'youse stay?' she said.

He muttered something polite
and disappointing: he could have reached out
and touched her, but he had somewhere to go.
She thanked him, calling him 'mister'
in a way that jarred him out of indifference.
She turned back to the mouth of the Underground.

Neither of them streetwise or proverbial-sly
she was trying this for the first time
and there was still some diffident fantasy
of spontaneous choice, that evaporated
when she thought of waking
to the colourless surprise of a man's back,

shelter meaning much until you have it
like a complicated dream of hunger:
bald towels hung at the bathroom door
like a pair of admonitory crows.
He could hear the rain in the sodden hills
around her shoulders, see the hidden scars

flower to open the contours of irony on her lips,
curling hard among the country syllables.
Like hunks of white bread drifting in pale ale

there were manly expectations in the air:
the best lacked all conviction,
and she knew where to find the rougher trade.

Asleep in their separate lives,
there was an inky silence over the water
but just below, small crustaceans
were busy with secrets and pincers,

using their shells to build settlements,
timescales, lessons and islands
eating all the while in minuscule detail.

Bees came and went on the sea
and they both swam in the whisper,
which in her dream became her father's shout.

# The choice of flowers

Through the rain's dissolute footsteps
the town's hum is a thing left on a stove,
beginning to cook on its own.
The call of a Boeing
is a fly that passes in the kitchen.
You are a warm light seen from the street,
but I am inside
and still surprised.
Something strange is happening.
I get off a bus in the wrong place
one midsummer dusk
and follow two strangers down a lane
under cascades of wild grass.
I am having an affair with fiction,
the passings, the shadow-life
of time misplaced.
The man didn't think of the woman
until it was too late.
He only thought of her when he was down,
and the thought uplifted him,
and when he saw her again he loved her,
and the years moved him.
And the woman disappeared,
there had been buttonholes and speeches
but on-one there knew
that where she began was much later
when bodies had filled out
and were prone to be comic vehicles
of dignity, courage or regret
and their beauty was a thing
that contained all these.

Someone waves from a life you didn't choose,
from a line of portholes
in a temporary structure,
and you realise the corridor you walk
is a life too.
The trick of familiarity
is a perverse trick,
you are buried in the present,
longing both to rise out of it
and into it.
An illusion of daffodils in the winter gloom
is an act of will or strangeness
and its light underneath your face
makes you look like a ghost.

# The Chiming at Trwyn Du

Brilliant as oiled plumage in hollows of sand
at first, the cars' paint
fades in the salt breeze
while their humans peel off into solitude.
The crest of the waves' surge is unbroken,
and the running of the silence is crowned
by the bell off Trwyn Du.
God's cry contracts to a hum
that fades in the current,
there, and there, he cannot
leave it alone, the loud
irregular call of a secretive bird.
There is no passage landward:
we watch, blessed, from the rocks
in the company of the deep-wrinkled mountains.

# Decision

I stood behind a white gate in a still orchard.
Through it, flies milled
and wheeled in the angle of sun
beneath a clasp of sycamores.
Higher, the wind caught saplings
and pulled them and turned every specific leaf
through the light.
In stillness, I watched its purpose
in many fingers pass.

Beads of dew were hung at my feet
in quick movements between
suspicions of movement.
From stillness, the slow gate
opened to the wind's purpose.

The protracted rasp of its hinge.

# For the Irish Sea

The sea is increasingly
a desperate metaphor:
the slimy creatures of the spirit
leave the shells of their body
recklessly in the sand;
when other people are beyond us
we retreat to the sea's
invulnerable dells.
Through swirling banks of weed
at their stations, tangle, dulse
and furbelows, through toothed wrack,
knotted wrack, channelled and spiral,
comes the radioactive word
released by the Secretary
for the Environment.
It churns the careless plankton
slowly with a dispassionate tail.
It is an experiment in barbarism,
a progress crowned.
Its fuel is knowledge
we cannot assimilate.
It has an origin to spoil.

# Optimism

Making and unmaking
in their hungry galleries of lacework,
the graceful chains of plankton surge
and dine on carbon-dioxide.

Lady Stanley's hundred-year-old
folly's now an observation tower
and it bristles with technology and pride.
Families queue on the stairs
to pour the special milk of their enjoyment
through a closed circuit camera,
the kind they use in supermarkets,
trained on observant lines of guillemots
that tip down from their shelves
to the sea's churning,
soldiers of optimism
where the surf breaks
among the hungry wilderness of cliffs.
The tower's been licked rough
with white weather-proof
after decades of neglect,
and now it stands out in the radial pulse
of the lighthouse below;
and as the beam sweeps off
and darkness deepens on the sea-pink
in the retina, the turret's white face brushes
with a passing glance of trawlers
that move out there
and are gone among the flashes
of white horse and gannet.
I struggle to persuade myself

that dereliction is made new,
having been once convinced merely
of the folly of its begetter.
There are photographs
of my babyhood in this place,
and the relatives numerous enough
to be visible to the seals
hooting and booming to each other
under the cliffs.
Columns of sunlight move
busy about plankton:
they are gardeners
that thin and rake with ultra-violet.
Look where we will,
the reflection off the rising sea
is volatile.

# Refugees

A man from Bethnal Green, that
pounded village, said I wrote
of London like some country mouse.
He laid claim, drily, to the voice
out of the dust along the sills
of his dilapidated block,
riding as surely as a dibbuk in a trough
behind the combing waves heaved
by his grandparents
like coal across the Baltic
where a pogrom or a near thing
harried them west to land him
lucky with impenetrable coolness
by a steam of notes rising
amplified between paving slabs,
the reassuring shudder
of a subterranean club.

We build our version of arrival
out of grandparents or giant figures
to make and explain us:

his were riding the wave of progress
towards away,
                    all effort and belief
in some fleeting credit of heaven
curved beyond them
since refusal often offends —
                    all backwash and filthy undertow
as far as they could bring the muddy
complications of their past

committed as wingless creatures
who believed and understood the principle
of flight, but lacked the mechanics
to stop or return.

As for him, he photographed a riot
quietly, till his camera was taken apart
in a flailing line of police:
he unravelled the film
for the marginal papers,
a memorable geometry of clubs
and perspex shields grown straight
as a stand of windows on the soul.

All are responsible for all
and we mean it in different ways.

At night the streets were filled
with a long migration,
they trailed up the pavement behind us
with their second-hand beginnings
in unruly suitcases
on a sluggish, ankle-deep tide.
Now others are stripped at airports
to their evaporating gratitude,
shoved back on planes
for Sri Lanka, Turkey or Iran —
it takes the duration
of an in-flight movie
to undo the nocturnal escape above the pass
the secret dried meat from a woman in the barn

the luck of playing dead behind the dead postman —
this is the ticket to the escape
on rewind to the Kalashnikov butt,
the disposal unit.

On Sunday mornings, in the indifferent
embrace of Stamford Hill, a stooped walk
for bagels symbolised arrival,
with the grandchild's little fingers
preserved in his, the grandfather's hand
preserved in what greater
                                        grace and favour —
the Sabbath night
had kept candles alight in the wind.

Later the little apostate cut himself
adrift by the sidelocks, and swam away
mutilated in the darkness
towards his revolution's precious
moment of innocence.
His grandfather saw otherwise:
'He was tied by lines of light
as far as he went, which was not so far:
they were like those lines of headlight
on a postcard he sent us
of the Champs Elysées.
I have smiled at progress now,
and try to make an altar at every step
I have understood.'

'Dibbuk' — in Yiddish, an evil and possessing spirit.

# Fluidity, Charmouth

A bare tree reaches over
from the cliff-edge mudslide:
dead of almost being airborne,
drawing up, drawing down
like a fishing rod,
a perch that has the air of carrion
for choughs that seethe up
from the marls below the lip.
Below, a skier on an avalanche,
there waits an ammonite
that glistens upward to the god's
eye that holds the scale of things.
The eye's blood-vessels
snag there in a branch.
A jug is pouring birds the other way.

# Misrule, Towyn, 1990

With a clatter, the sea pushes
its tongue through the letterbox.
It does not empty or relieve itself.
The Axminster rises towards the ceiling,
passing a barometer half way up.

*This is my home and I'm having it back*
*from the sea: swilling up to the front room sill*
*and window-frame, newly reglossed*
*in duck-egg blue, fourteen years of marriage.*
*Grateful to find there are knickers*
*intact on the top shelf: one pair fresh*
*as rising dough on the hearth*
*and I'm ready to meet my maker.*

Hers is a small house
in a silent gallery of snow,
in a plastic capsule won from a cracker,
broken soon: a hermit crab
darts below the swirling fall of sand
among the surging levities of beach-plastic
and the shoes that feel life returning
in the bedroom.
The rattle of shingle
is uniform and triumphant
across the kitchen floors of Towyn.

On a roof anchored uncertainly with planks,
there were ovals of grey ice
on blue plastic sheeting
like lakes from a plane in blue mountains
as I lean down from an early meal.

My son asks
if it was like this in Atlantis,
a little water
riding together suddenly
over the flat of his hand
as he lowers it in the bath,
knocking the houses over, like this.

I must have been twelve or thereabouts
when I pored through the atlas,
speculating what would be left of the uplands
if the sea reached six hundred feet,
recording it all meticulously
as the sea blustered
not far from the door:
the West Siberian Plain,
the basin of the Ganges and the Brahmaputra,
the Fens, the North European Plain,
most of Cheshire —
was it the fury of clouds I wanted
or simply disorder,
was it a sad end,
was it a just desert
or the little death
that sets a story in motion?
The strong winds rage along the isobars
and people begin not to notice
how it plucks and tears at awnings,
raging at bars,
perhaps more that it did before.

On the way to work,
I noticed how the buildings
loitered in the street,
how I could have stopped
and watched anything happen:

*it was a sharp cold day,*
*people ran to the river bank*
*as a shack approached*
*and floated slowly past:*
*at the open back a boy and a small girl,*
*between them a dog with its back to the water,*
*the boy taking pulls of a cigarette,*
*the girl holding the tip of the dog's tail*
*between her fingers in the same way,*
*pale and very concentrated.*
*We were left gawping.*

*We felt our ways*
*upstream and down*
*for something familiar.*

*But now you cannot retreat as far as the sea*
*you belong to*
*because it will come for you.*

# The shooting of Levellers
# Burford, 1649

From the roof of Burford Church
that served its turn as prison
and grandstand for an exemplary killing,
the final purity of the starlight:
first an idea, yoked with violence together,
then broken up into uncontrollable particles
as in the rasping, visible breath
among three hundred
of Anthony Sedley, sixteen-forty-nine,
prisner, who cut the many short
diagonal scores of his name in the font.
The fires of Cromwell and Fairfax
among the tombs
were will-o'the-wisps grown monstrous,
mocking the name of Sedley
as it drained with the first light,
waiting in all his physical detail,
in the biting of his lip
for the names of the dead.
Sedley, spared:
chosen, Cornet Thompson, Corporal Perkins,
Private Church.
They had no memorial:
Cromwell spoke quietly to them,
this was marked
before they were shot.
In his hurry
he began to cut 'Athony',
and had to go over it.

He had scratched a secret presence,
given time, in the naming of children,
in the renouncing of the vain
pomp and glory of the world
with all covetous desires of the same
and the carnal desires of the flesh,
so that thou wilt not follow
nor be led by them,
to be on the safe side
for Liberty cannot be provided for
in a general sense
if property be preserved.
His balls contracted
for no wonder he hath enemies,
the hairs on his back
raised in each particular.

He walked away unmarked,
his stomach ploughed with fear
across watermeadows,
turning in his mind
the bird that will only fly
inside a jar
that awaits a shattering,
a reckoning,
the unbearable rush of freedom:
his name without a gravestone,
in a font.

# Chips

Was this going to sell the beer
or the car?

He drove through the rough streets
in an endearing light
of sunset and elderly brick.
His features were delicate
yet incisive, like the car.
His was an integrated
but far-reaching life
with a sliver of unease,
enough sadness to give him depth
but not enough to make him unenviable.
He was driving to the Soldier's Return,
wearing a quality scarf thrown
with timing on a well-cut tweed
to find his father where he left him,
non-verbal, waiting for a pint awkwardly.
He got the pint,
among silenced friends,
a smooth one.
They recognised him as he sat beside his Dad
and looked ahead and they supped.
The car's metallic glint outside,
his capsule with Vivaldi
waiting on the brick road.
It could have been transmuted, easily,
from Warrington to Mantua.

We smiled throughout the cinema.
We felt good about ourselves,
or what we could be, could have been,
or about someone we had known,
not quite ourselves. And why not?
The Dad's face broke into a smile,
or was about to.

At the post-mortem
the team from Marketing
were breasting the tape again,
riding the crest,
surfing the shit —
and why not?
The creative one
slapped his desk with pleasure.

When the chips are down
whose will they be?

# Old hope

On its arc the bottle
from the woman in the white hat
swings out
and encapsulates
a thought of thrift and waste.
Behind it
trails the sun and rivermist
and the soil that made the grape:
the growing falls away
before the clang and shatter
of its green hip
on the new-named hull.

The vessel's triggered off the slipway
like a pinball sprung hesitantly
downwards
and unable to pull back,
recalling how night turns away from dusk
irretrievably, and how a swell
undoes the calm:
the men in overalls
make the illusion work
hidden as fish with their hammers
down there
on the metal-rich alluvium

and our idea of scale
founders
as the big chocks fly
and, bobbing,
all those hollow tons
displace the river

and then rise
like the grooved moons of a docker's bum
above his denim
with a woman at the primum mobile
in white gloves in a tableau
on a scaffold with the Mayor.

It just keeps going
through a tunnel under cloud
bolting for a sheen of north
then an impossible Homeric blue
the men in overalls will stand beneath.

# Murder

The wreaths,
the bloom faded of red stains
on the fouled pavement
under the green door;
the clean machete with plastic ribbons round it
like roadworks,
the plain-clothesmen
hatching something in a leather jacket,
maggots for bait perhaps
or the unlikely reductive process
of their logic
under a brow of white knuckle.
Criminals or young people
had been passing the crack in plant tubs:
the police comically just missed every time.
The noise of the club, through repetition,
gathers mass, it is not joy,
it is smoke on the point
of becoming solid
with figures trapped inside
gesticulating for a future
where they have the power
at least to be dangerous to others.
The sky an afterthought,
an irrelevance, a parasol
keeping its distance,
passing by on the other side.

But in the dawn,
across the alley from the stacked crates
of empties,
hundreds of sparrows chattering
in a Russian vine draped over a factory
reminded me of a school canteen.
Let that be his memorial,
whoever he was.

# Shamanism, Dalston

In the snarl-up you generate cursory images
for a boy who plays with his remote.
He is a midge that can change currents at will,
his mind darts and flickers on the channels
of boredom. Your roots have spread behind the wheel
and the shining trails on your windscreen.
From behind your demister
you watch the schoolboys
dealing in the doorways of the supermarket.
With their rocks of crack
they're an extension to the national gallery.

Behind a skip off Gillett Street
big boys on little stolen bikes
pick up their envelopes.
There's a sense of industry and purpose
and a young shaman behind the wheel
of a big car thinks he's driving.
He slips on his other skin
and takes on the illness of others
like the illness of a giant corporation
like something forgotten
deliberately with videos.

In the grip and thunder of music
under narcotic overhangs
his strides are disproportionate
through the market's hills
of litter people pick among.
A mile away, the little dealers
with a habit flare in the washrooms
of the glass towers
above the Provisionals' bombs.

They are the flames in desert wells
from forty thousand feet over Libya:

so they can watch over us,
they do not sleep.
We are unaware of their white noise.
The shifting of currency is linked
through the darkness of the land between the lights
where lightless farms boil dry
like overheated radiators.
All the powers were independent
in the Shaman's world:
yet the crop was distributed in the alley
where they had a boy to look after the cars.

No need to understand the needs of goats,
anywhere. No need to be stacking shelves
and losing face. There was no such thing
as society. There is not much to be heard
for the clacking of credit cards
in the bushes. Your head is razored
to the bone, telling you the skin
is a brief tent draped over rifts.
Stalled in the traffic, you realise
you and those on your screen
have windows down to the pavement.

# Giving them what for

## 1

### County Court

It's the incompetence
of repossession that sticks:
the sometimes conscious absurdity
worn on a sleeve,
the incredulity.
Estate managers tanned
and tied for the day —
they are ill-rehearsed
and their figures are wrong
but the responsibility
sits easy with them.
A barrister stoops
above the mill of peoples,
angrier than his client
to find himself here,
shouting questions at a Greek
to make him understand.
A woman with the Koran
has a look of fearful delicacy
aware of every flicker
of nonsense,
every downward pull
of stale tobacco and sweat.
Sending cheques to her mother
in North Africa,
working for her doctorate
she doesn't belong here:
there's one every morning,
a moment of satisfying clemency.

A fallen advocate from Pakistan
has a vest beneath his shirt
that reads 'Yellow Pages'.
A woman with her son and her friend
are giggling along the pew.
Where the wages of sin are,
there are naughty bits.
Eviction's like losing your blouse
on a horse, but (anything legal
considered) she might flash her tits
at the testy Registrar with mottled hands.
Her son says he'll clean cars
on Saturdays.
An Irishman stamps from the Court
shouting 'Ah well, Oi'm off to Choina'.
This is a private statement
and it's somehow right
that nobody understands.

## 2

### The Leaving Do

There was a murmur of envy
as you announced the abandonment
of your career, because
there no longer seemed any point
to managing homelessness,
to containment
of the need for containment.
A curtain swayed by the French window
that opened on the devious yard
of possibility, with its sky.
You left a roomful of appreciative drinkers,
and progress,
and routine,
and the sharper creases and the shoe-polish
under the table.

By the exercise of nous
and the firm look you conjured
from somebody's mother,
your job was to avoid
the need to sort the feckless
from the stricken:
but when the chips were down,
to cast them out.
You had to dress up to do it.
Those you had managed
expected little of you:
it was for this shame you were paid.
Now those who have the character
will be battle-hardened

and ready to rule and draw hard lines.
And those who complain
will be cast out beyond the pork-barrel
to the further margins
with no regular buses,
disloyal, foolish and hungry still.
In Eastern Europe, people believe
because they must
that the homeless camp out
through choice in the West.

Who chose the verminous sleeping bag
and the whispering lung?

The friends you met
coming the other way,
   resigned to victory,
   their dispatches memorised
      or making their plans in silence
      on the up escalator
took a stumbling feint
into the U-bend of the future
before emergence,
   holding their bunch of violets
   up like an Olympic flame,
   burning away the gases,
brushing the wet hair and the lost words
out of their eyes.

# Nearness

I have trailed you in several senses,
hunger, acolyte, waif, trudge,
in the wood the figure following,
with my finger in the afternoon that found you,
vapour trail gathering its plane,
defining what you would have done
without me in the wide spaces,
among the possibilities
grazing with their open mouths
and their numberless tongues
running over you.
You look round in a flash of colour
the fish swim toward and are gone,
then I know I'm the waiting land,
the other shore that does not follow.

## Unwritten chapters

In which the audience doesn't warn him
In which he is in heaven, and for eternity he doesn't love the
people he thought he did
In which every cloud has a blind horse
In which he does not know that a cloud is rising behind him
In which he jumps over the fire all night, and is sick in the end
In which he is taken in to the architecture of the trout
In which the poets write better history than the historians,
but it is not the same
In which he cannot do things he knows he can do
In which the most familiar room cannot be entered
In which most daylight has a velvet ear
In which it's a short wolf that sees an ant

# Belonging

I was flying.
The ground was silent under dry leaves.
I was tenuous
and the stars were quiet in their intimate smoke.
From a distance they turned systematically,
I understood the mathematics.
Some were spent
in a fall of cinders
beyond the dune.
At another speed
I passed the years
turning in their long fall;
there were forebears
I could nearly touch.
Not having known where down is
I am grounded.
As a roof-tree
burrows toward the sky
and a leaf turns through the light,
stones come apart
with soft cracks.

# The doors of the year, well done

Up Balls Pond Road the turkey's
speeding past the window
where the Eyyup Ercan Mustafa Brothers'
sausage in batter's left for dead.
Straining through the door-frame
full of ebullience,
it takes to the cognac like after-shave
in readiness for the solitary honours
of the oven.
                    Stuffed
with prunes and apricots
it'll agree to anything
like some half-remembered uncle.
Our cat Snowflake bites
digits at the edge of madness,
faced with the deadpan requiescat
of the sealed container
where the turkey slumbers
like Sir Walter Raleigh, his ultimate night
only fruitless this one.

At the thought of its acned gooseflesh
are we less implausible, alive
and unplucked of our dignities?
Was it stuffed with fishmeal for Jesus?

Gorging is deeply ingrained
to force the window of the New Year
and to make the Sun come pink again
blushing a few minutes above the horizon
the colour of a hung turkey
to help us sleep easy now
towards the buds in the snow.

May the last supper
with its judicious shower of friends
last long, the turkey flushed and full of itself
and the Queen allowed in again
after all these years
to say that harmless parody;
may we forgive our parents
as we forgive ourselves
within the bottles
of our sloped shoulders.
May we grow politic, mellow
and forgive our little replicas
and the poorer years:
but first, this morning,
the expected spoiling of toys,
the glow of obtrusive joy,
the hopping from foot to foot
at the grey crack of dawn
as we insist on the revenge
of the watched kettle
before the grating
tear of paper and the crows
of delight by the black grate.
And awake on the gradient of morning
the root vegetables
coming smooth in my hand
amid your fury of industrious love.

Like a minute of impending snow
the turkey in the oven
darkens and whitens.

# Ciudadela, 1991

Under the stretched skin of the houses,
under the whitewash
facing the sharp sun over the rocks,
under the sheet binding the jawbone
the dreams are obscured.
The televisions are off
like cagebirds with blankets over them.
Wakers turn to reach
familiar points
of reassurance and pleasure
where they are to be found.
Aimless hymns are gathered into the sky
from streets deep in shadow
where the smell of the baker
and the early bicycles remain.
The first components of the town's
prayer of noise under the sun
are cocks and mopeds and the secret
plume of a fart under the sheet.

At eleven the sun holds my head
in its grip,
a thing detached in its lap:
there is no comfort of reference
in the quickness of the lizard
or the sardine or even the bells.

Take me in, to the upturned boat
of stone on the horizon,
the fresh breeze, the thanks of green
in the glaciated valley,
the hand on me of that.

By one, the fish are a triumph,
running through the glades.
I watch them till the water
rises in my mask,
the little schools that graze
and synchronise, dart
and flock in the grainy diminished light.

The sun's a watery ripple
on the surface of the ceiling at four.
Street voices surround me like cold air.
The ceiling fan draws me up.
Blue-white legs have stirred the plaster
and are propelled out of vision;
their scrotum or light-bulb
is a towed anchor.

Dusk: a man disgorged safely
on the sand, if he can find the right sea.
The rhythm of the other sea in the shallows
does the moon's breathing.

A couple are up to their shoulders
in the bay: the other sea
explores their limbs
fast together
as tongues in secret explore each other.

# Tŷ Newydd

A supple, determined V of geese
follows the line of the surf,
knowing September into the stiff wind:
flecks of whitecaps above them
reach to the indistinct
hinge of the sky.

I listened for that hinge:
my whisper came back to me
like the surf across the railway line
and up the hill, but it was busy, busy,
building hypotheses,
stakes for the heart.

The memory of power
brushed me, and I thought
of the day I first dressed myself
and I stood up
and surveyed the distance to the floor
that pushed up towards me.

Then the paradox of generosity
called by
in a daydream of a place
where people lock the door
and leave the key outside
in welcome to the unexpected guest —

or — with the stillness at my back
as I turn away from the empty room —
locking the inside in.
So I climbed away:
there was a delicious cold sweat
under my shirt for the wind to play on.

There were green shoots among burned heather
in dense cloud, and I heard wings:
they were the flutter of brown paper
unwrapped in another room:
they were the poetry shut in,
with misgivings, a concealed offer.

# Acknowledgements

The first three sections are taken from *Anglesey Material* (Rex Collings, 1980), *Civilised Airs* (Poetry Wales Press, 1984), and *Uncontrollable Fields* (Seren Books, 1990).

Some of the new poems have appeared in *Planet, Poetry Wales, New Welsh Review,* and *Cyphers* (Eire).

Other poems previously appeared in *Stand, Literary Review, Anglo-Welsh Review, Gallery, Poetry Wales, Tribune, Argo, City Limits, New Wales, Element 5, Long Pen, Radical Wales,* and the *New Welsh Review.* Much of *Anglesey Material* and some other poems were broadcast on Radio 3.

Poems from this selection have also appeared in the *Poetry Book Society Anthology* (1990), (Hutchinson), *Anglo-Welsh Poetry 1480-1980* (Poetry Wales Press), *The Bright Field* (contemporary poetry from Wales, Carcanet 1991), and other anthologies.